NIGHT

VISIONS

GOD REVEALS HIMSELF THROUGH
DREAMS

NIGHT

VISIONS

GOD REVEALS HIMSELF THROUGH DREAMS

GRETA JAMES

Glimpse of Glory
CHRISTIAN BOOK PUBLISHING

CONTENTS

ACKNOWLEDGMENTS

To my Heavenly Father:

First and foremost, I would like to thank You, Father God, for Your many blessings. I am truly honored that You decided to use me as a vessel to write this book. You could have chosen someone else for a time such now. I am forever grateful it was me.

To my daughter:

I want to thank my beautiful daughter, Camille Miller, for understanding why I needed the time to myself to write this book. You are such a precious gift that I am honored to teach, nurture, love, inspire, guide, etc. You are the best. Mommy loves you.

To my sister:

I want to thank my beautiful sister, Quenshelia James, for encouraging me to "just write the book." You are such a great inspiration in my life. Your words gave me the push I needed to get started on this book.

To my friends:

I want to thank Eileen Horton for being a devoted friend, and for even being a mother figure in my life at times. I want to thank Loretta Andrews for being the big sister I never had and for speaking positive words into my life long before this book.

To my sisters and brothers from Freedom Fridays:

I would also like to thank my sisters and brothers who were frequently at Freedom Fridays, especially Mrs. Anita Jefferson who spoke to me about procrastination before writing this book, and for also pointing me in the right direction. Thank you, Laquita Hankins, for hosting Freedom Fridays; it was during those events that I discovered what I am supposed to write about. The next Freedom Friday will be held at my house.

To the dreamers:

I encourage you to always journal or simply write down what you dream of becoming in life. The Bible tells us to

"Write the vision and make it plain…" (Habakkuk 2:2). God will reveal things to you concerning your future, and sometimes He will reveal those things through dreams.

INTRODUCTION

As you read this book, you will begin to have a greater understanding of dreams that are given to you by God and how to handle them. Most, if not all, people have dreams. It is a blessing to be a dreamer. It is also a blessing to have the gift of interpretation because it helps you to gain a better understanding of your dreams.

Dreaming is one way God speaks to us, His children. "Dreams are called God's secret weapon or the sleep language of God." He will reveal many things to you through dreams. Anything He shows you in dreams are going to be supported by His Word, even if it is a dream to warn you to go in a different direction to avoid trouble. Anything He says to you is also going to be supported by His Word. The Word of God says, "All Scripture is God-breathed and is useful for teaching, rebuking, correcting and training in righteousness, so that the man of God may be thoroughly equipped for every good work."

God is not One who will contradict Himself, so if you have a dream (nightmare) that strips your peace, joy, sanity…and it does not line up with the sweet nature of God, then you should "cast down those imaginations and every high thing that will even try to exalt itself against the knowledge of God…"

I want you to know that God is not the source of any negative or demonic dream. You must learn to cancel every assignment of darkness, and also every demonic force that will try to come through your dreams, immediately after you wake from having an evil dream.

You can have confidence in knowing that you will certainly find strength and hope in God-given dreams.

MY DREAMS

I would like to share with you a series of dreams that I can remember having from childhood up to my adult life. All of those dreams that I had were significant to me. I considered some of them to be prophetic dreams; that means they did happen according to what was revealed and shared by God.

، I can remember the very first time I had a dream that was significant. I was about seven or eight years old. My brother Charles had a brand new car that he took pride in keeping clean. One particular night, I dreamed that he had a terrible wreck and completely totaled

15

his car. I woke up and immediately told my mother about the dream that I had.

Later that morning someone came to our house and informed us of another young man named Charles who was involved in a car accident the night before, and his new car was totaled. My mother looked at me a bit bewildered after learning of what happened that night.

In 2002, I dreamed that I was sitting in church during a Sunday morning service. I remember when my pastor stood up and said, "God is going to use someone here today to motivate others to give." I looked around and wondered who God was going to use, not even realizing that it would be me. When I looked at this one particular man, the

16

Holy Spirit spoke to me and directed me to tell him to give and that he would receive it back in the form of a 10-fold blessing within four days. God also instructed me to tell a young lady to give, too.

After having that dream, the very next day I immediately called my pastor and told him about the dream. He encouraged me to share the dream with the congregation during the next church service. He later told me that he was in need of finances to pay a utility bill. The utility company was supposed to go to his house the Friday of that same week to cut the meter off, but they did not have to go after all. Because of my obedience to God, my

17

pastor's need was met; his utility service was not interrupted.

I want to tell you about another dream that I had in the month of September 2008. I dreamed of a couple who had been dating for quite some time. The young man (I will call him Mark) decided it was time to propose to his fiancé', and he did it in such a beautiful way. I was very excited for the couple and truly did wish nothing but the best for them.

However, sometime later, in the month of March 2009, I had another dream that they would not be getting married and it was because he had been cheating. I thought that dream was from the devil, and I did not want to speak what I dreamed about aloud in the atmosphere. I only wrote about it in my journal that I used to record dreams. I also prayed that that dream would not manifest.

Unfortunately that dream became a reality. Not only was he cheating on his fiancé, but the other woman that he was involved with conceived a baby. The young lady who he had proposed to was so devastated after hearing about what happened. Needless to say, they did not get married. This dream was evident that God will reveal some things for us to pray about but not for us to reveal to others.

I remember having another dream that I believe was used to prepare or warn. It was in the month of April 2013 when I woke from that very disturbing dream. I dreamed that a particular female church member had died from having a brain aneurism, leaving her husband a widower. That dream left me worried.

I felt led to tell a certain prayer warrior who attended the same church as I did. After I shared the dream with her, we began to pray for that lady. About a month or so later, I learned that the prayer warrior who prayed with me collapsed in the pulpit at another church. She had a brain aneurism.

I immediately knew why I was led to tell her. She and I had been praying… not even knowing that those prayers would actually be for her. I believe this was a test for her. Soon after she recovered from having the brain aneurism, she admitted that she did not think the lady who she and I had been praying for even liked her. I must tell you that God certainly works in mysterious ways.

I cannot forget to tell you about the dream that I had in the month of May 2013. That particular dream was about a female minister (and her husband) who attended the same church as I did. She and her husband decided to move to another state. Some of the members and I expressed that we would miss her. I still believe that she and her husband supposed to be residing in Huntsville, Alabama.

Later that year, September 21 to be exact, I had another dream pertaining to her. In that dream one of the elders at

21

the church came to me and said that he saw a minister at the store in a drunken, backslidden state. All of a sudden I saw a yard where the grass was extremely high, and then a large lawnmower that appeared to be moving, cutting down a section of the grass to reveal a garden tool. Then, three faces were revealed. It was the minister's daughter and her granddaughter and one of the prayer intercessors from the church that I attended.

I was a bit confused after having that dream. I am actually still seeking God for answers to that dream. I believe that He will certainly uncover and reveal whatever is hidden.

On September 22, 2015, around 4:04 p.m. (this was a day vision), I had a dream that my daughter Camille and I were riding in the back seat of a car with a young girl who really seemed unfamiliar to me. I did not recognize who she was, but the fact that we were riding in the same car indicated we were somewhat acquainted.

While traveling to our destination, I looked out of the windshield of the car and saw what appeared to be a snake. I thought that I was having an open vision but the snake was actually in the car with us. It was between the two front seats below the radio, right next to the gear stick, moving in a downward motion on the driver's side. It was hiding under some white napkins... It was a thin, black snake, but it was camouflaged by those white napkins that was lying by the gear stick. I immediately screamed, "Snake!"

The young lady who was driving quickly moved her right foot to accelerate the gas, and then the snake bit her on that foot after she moved it. I immediately dialed 911 on my cell phone for help. The young lady pulled the car over into a service station and, before she could park the car, the paramedics had arrived. My daughter and I got out of the car, and then we saw the snake again. It was trying to hide under the white napkins, but we were still able to see it.

God gave the revelation that the snake was a person who was portraying to be a saint ("a holy person, one who is set apart"). This was a man who had

24

been attending church posing as a saint, but he was really a snake in disguise.

This man was involved with the young lady who was bitten by the snake. The pain that she suffered from the snake bite was a representation of the "pain" that he would inflict upon her if the relationship between the two of them continued.

Finally, I want to share this last dream with you. On July 11, 2016 at 5:30 p.m., I dreamed about a fellow coworker. He managed a group of boys who were in a gospel choir. The boys were all in an auditorium getting ready to sing at a musical event. I saw a lady there who once stayed in my home for a while. She was there to support the leader of the choir. There was also another young lady at the event. She appeared to be the lead singer of the choir.

The following day, around 10:00 a.m., God gave me a revelation about that dream. He revealed that will He often send His disciples ("one who embraces and assists in spreading the teachings of another.") to places in a pair to minister and teach His Word.

I want you to know that the devil is sending more demons to places to combat the work of the Lord. He has added another component to try to defeat God and His children. The devil's mission is to "kill, steal and destroy."

The woman who used to stay in my home needed to be delivered from divination, but she refused it. She has been going to various places to search for what only God can give. She feels that she cannot go to church, so she has made new connections…She and the male leader of the gospel choir are both deceivers.

I believe that that dream was to warn me not to be in the company of those two people when they are singing at any particular church or venue.

27

NIGHT VISIONS

CHAPTER 1

THE PURPOSE OF DREAMING

According to Merriam-Webster's dictionary, the word dream is defined as a series of thoughts, images, and sensations occurring in a person's mind during sleep. Many of us have dreams, or what I refer to as night visions. All dreams do not occur during the night. Some dreams can also occur during the day when one is awake; these are known as day visions.

As I stated before, dreaming is one of the many ways God uses to speak to

29

us. God has to show some of us important things while we are asleep; otherwise, some of us will miss what He is trying to reveal to us because we lead busy lives. He knows that when we are asleep, we are in a relax mode and our spirits are more inclined to hear what He has to say.

The Word of God shares with us many stories of people who were dreamers. Jacob was one of those people. In the book of Genesis 28:12-16, it says, "And he dreamed, and behold a ladder set up on the earth, angels ascended and descended. And, behold, the Lord stood above it, and said, I am the Lord, God of Abraham thy father, and the God of Isaac: the land whereon thou liest, to thee will I

30

give it, and to thy seed; And thy seed shall be as the dust of the earth, and thou shalt spread abroad to the west, and to the east, and to the north, and to the south: and in thee and in thy seed shall all the families of the earth be blessed. And, behold, I am with thee, and will keep thee in all places whither thou goest, and will bring thee again into this land; for I will not leave thee, until I have done that which I have spoken to thee of. And Jacob awaked out of his sleep, and he said, surely, the Lord is in this place; and I knew it not."

Joseph, Mary's husband, was also a dreamer. In the book of Matthew 1:20, it says, "But as he considered these things, behold an angel of the Lord appeared to him in a dream saying

Joseph, son of David, do not fear to take Mary as your wife, for that which conceived in her is from the Holy Spirit."

Also, let's not forget about Pilot's wife. In the book of Matthew 27:19, it says, "When he was sitting on the judge's seat, his wife sent unto him saying, have thou nothing to do with that just man: for I have suffered many things this day in a dream because of him."

And, last but not least, Pharaoh even dreamed. The Bible says that he was standing by the Nile River when seven cows sleek and fat appeared and grazed among the weeds. "After those seven ugly and gaunt cows appeared and stood beside those on the river bank ate the seven sleek fat cows, then Pharaoh woke up…"

As we can see from each of these dreams, they were all significant. I want you to understand that there is a message in every dream.

Some dreams are meant to…

Warn You

When you wake up every day, you expect for good and positive things to happen to and for you, and also for your family and friends. Sometimes in life you will encounter unexpected things, and those things may not always be favorable. Some of those unexpected things are attacks from the devil, but God will even warn you of those things in a dream. Yes, He is gracious enough to show you those things that may not appear to be favorable.

The good news is that even when unexpected things happen to you, you can have full assurance that everything will still work together for your good, according to Romans 8:28.

Prepare You

Sometimes God will reveal to you in a dream where He is taking you. You were already "destined for greatness" before your mother gave birth to you. I want you to understand that each of us has to go through the preparation process in life. You cannot arrive at a certain place that God has destined for you to be without preparation.

34

The preparation process is usually steps we all have to follow. When you have those dreams of God giving you a glimpse of where He is taking you, He will provide specific details only for that particular step because He doesn't want you to get ahead of Him and miss what He has for you. Preparation is a part of His plan for your life.

Remind You of His Promises

God may have promised you a particular thing, but He did not tell you when it would manifest and, because it has not happened yet, you may feel that it is not going to happen.

Sometimes when you are at the brink of giving up because you feel like the promise is null and void, God will

35

remind you of that promise in a dream. The Word of God says, "For all the promises of God in Him are yea, and in Him Amen, unto the glory of God by us." (2 Corinthians 1:20). His Word will give you assurance that every promise will be fulfilled in your life. God does not default on His promises. He keeps every one of them.

I encourage you to have confidence in knowing that He will do whatever it is that He says He will do for you, according to His Word. Keep your faith and trust God.

36

CHAPTER 2

SHARING YOUR DREAMS

It is not uncommon to share your dreams with other people. Your desire to share your dream with others is often intensified when that dream is "all that and more". What I mean by this is that if you have that awesome dream where God is giving you a glimpse of a blessing that you are about to receive, a promotion that you are about to receive, a financial increase...you have an accelerated desire to share it.

Oftentimes we will find ourselves sharing our dreams with people who

37

are close to us, and that includes our family members and our friends. But sometimes those people we are excited to share our dreams with are the same ones who are not so excited about some of the things that God may reveal to us in our dreams. Like, you know, getting that promotion that God promised you will obtain.

I would like to direct your attention to the story in the Holy Bible about Joseph, the son of Jacob. He was excited to share with his brothers what God showed him in one of his dreams. In the book of Genesis 37:6-8 it says, "...Listen to the dream I had. We were tying up bundles of grain out in the field. Suddenly my bundle rose and stood up straight and your bundles gathered around my bundle and bowed down to it. His brothers said to him, "Do you intend to reign over us? Will you actually rule us?" And they hated him all the more because of his dream and what he had said."

God showed Joseph in that dream that he would be in an important leadership position and his brothers would have to submit to him. His brothers did not like the fact that he would someday lead them, so they all conspired against him and tried to kill him by throwing him into a pit. (Read Genesis 37:18-20).

I want you to know that every dream is not meant to be shared, not even with the people you think are in your corner. Some dreams are meant just for you;

that is why God only showed you. If He wanted others to know every detail about what He showed you in a dream, believe me, He would have shown them too.

Before sharing your dreams, I would like to encourage you to…

Get God's Permission

You should never find it strange to get God's permission on any matter in your life, even something as simple as whether or not you should share a dream. While you may think that dreaming is a small thing, it can be a huge thing to God if you share what He revealed to you without even asking

Him whether or not you should even share it.

God finds honor in the fact that you will not only seek Him about revelation concerning a dream you may have, but to even ask Him if you should share it with anyone is adoration for Him.

Wait Until the Appointed Time to Share

The Bible tells us that even "the vision is for an appointed time." (Read Habakkuk 2:3). Since God is the head of all of our lives and the One who gives us visions and dreams; He has a set time for things to happen in our lives.

He has a set time for you to receive miracles. He has a set time for you to

41

receive blessings. He has a set time for you to be promoted. He has a set time for you to experience His promises. He even has a set time for you to share your dreams and visions.

Sometimes when you do things and share things outside of that appointed time, it can cause unnecessary delays in your life.

Only Share with Who God Tells You to Share with

You must be careful who you share your dreams with. I want you to know that it can easily be of harm to you if you share your dreams with the wrong people. I want you to know that people in your family can be the wrong ones to share your dreams with. Remember, again, Joseph shared a dream he had with his own brothers, and they hated him even the more.

You must realize that everyone you know or think that is for you is not happy about where God is taking you. You cannot be so quick to share your good news with them. Be careful. Some of your family members and friends, and even some of the people you attend church with will conspire against you and try to harm you, just as Joseph brothers did him.

NIGHT VISIONS

CHAPTER 3

UNDERSTANDING YOUR DREAMS

The Word of God shares with us the importance of getting understanding, even so much that it says in Proverbs 4:7, "...with all thy getting, get understanding." If you lack having understanding about something, you can misconstrue whatever it may be, including a dream that you might have.

God will specifically show you certain things in a dream. Some dreams are shown in two, three and four parts, and yet they are all apart of the same message that is intended for you.

God will provide clarity to your dreams through...

The Gift of Interpretation

God knows that many of us who dream do not always understand the meaning of our dreams; that is why He gives some of us the precious gift of interpretation—this is a spiritual gift to help you understand what He shows you in a dream. If you cannot interpret a dream, He will direct you to someone who He has gifted to interpret dreams.

I would like to direct your attention to Joseph again. Remember, Joseph was a dreamer, but he also had the gift of interpretation. In Genesis 40:12-13, it refers to a dream he interpreted for someone who shared it with him. "This is what it means," Joseph said to him. "The three branches are three days. Within three days Pharaoh will lift up your head and restore you to your position and you will put Pharaoh's cup in his hand, just as you used to do when you were his cupbearer."

Prayer

"The effectual fervent prayers of a righteous man (and woman) availeth much." (James 5:16). When you pray to God about anything, He will answer you. God loves when you petition Him about things that matter to you.

47

Just like some situations can lead you to pray to God for guidance, etc., some dreams that you have will make you seek Him for understanding. Some dreams are straightforward, and others are a little more detailed; therefore, those dreams will require a better and clearer understanding.

I have learned through the many dreams that I have had how important it is to pray to our Heavenly Father for revelation knowledge. I have had to pray about many of those dreams because I wanted to understand the message that He was conveying to my spirit.

I can assure you that God will never leave you confused after you have had a dream, wondering what the meaning of the dream was. He will make sure you understand the purpose of it.

Prophecy

God will also confirm and provide understanding of a dream through a prophet or a prophetess. This is "a person chosen to speak for God and to guide people..." God communicates often to His prophets and prophetesses through dreams.

You may have a dream that you do not quite understand and, all of a sudden, you may be at church or in a grocery story, or just running errands on any given day, and God may use a total stranger (a prophet or prophetess) to say something to you about a dream that you have been praying to Him

49

about. You see, God will ensure that you have all the clarity you need about a dream, or anything else.

CHAPTER 4

JOURNALING YOUR DREAMS

If you dream often, it is very important to keep a journal or notebook within your reach so that you keep track of your dreams, and the date and time of a dream, if possible.

It is my own personal belief that God wants us to keep a journal to record our dreams since this is one of the ways He shares with us and reveals to us what He wants us to know. I believe it shows Him that what He has to say to us is important and that it will not be taken for granted.

By journaling your dreams, it allows you to...

Remember What You Dreamed About

Every dream that God is the source of is valuable and, by recording that dream, you will always remember when and what He shared. Of course, you will need to keep your journal throughout the years just in case you ever need to revisit one of the dreams you had.

See All the Details of Your Dreams on Paper

When you write down the details of a dream that you have, you can easily reference what was shared in that dream if you decide to pick up your journal and read it one day.

You will also get to see the bigger picture when you have it all on paper; this makes your dream have more life and meaning to it.

Remind God of What He Showed You

I believe that God wants you to remind Him of something that He shows you in a dream. He wants you to know that He is more than able to perform whatever good thing that He shows you or promises you in a dream. When you remind Him of what He showed you...dream, it makes Him accountable to His Word.

NIGHT VISIONS

CHAPTER 5

MANIFESTATION OF YOUR DREAMS

One thing to remember is that if God told you that He would do something for you, or revealed to you in a dream what you will become, where He is taking you, a blessing that He will reward you with…or anything else of godly substance, you can believe that He will definitely follow through and honor His Word.

God will never speak a lie. Every Word that proceeds out of His mouth is true. I want you to know that God's

55

Word is also pure, sure and it will never return to Him void. Again, if He said it, if He revealed it to you in a dream, if He promised it, then you can be assured that it will be so—it will manifest.

When those awesome dreams start manifesting, you should…

Thank God

God deserves to be thanked every single day; for all that He has done and will do for you. Just to see a dream manifest is a sign of His awesome power, so you should not only thank Him for bringing something to fruition that He revealed to you in a dream, but for His goodness, for having you on His mind and for loving you enough to speak to you, and even comfort you through a dream.

Have More Confidence in His Plans for Your Life

It is exciting to know that God has a plan for my and your life. You may have a dream where He will reveal a portion of His plan for your life. When you see some of the plan manifest, you will not only be confident in His great plan...but you will be more excited about the things that He has yet to reveal because of this: "For I know the plans I have for you, declares the Lord. They are plans to prosper you and not to harm you, plans to give you hope and a future."

Be More Accountable

When God performs that great thing that He said that He would do, then you should be more accountable to Him. He should be able to trust you even the more. He should be able to count on you to obey Him and follow through with the instructions He gives you.

Be Strengthen in Your Faith

It is not always easy to have faith when you are going to tough and rough times, dealing with the cares of life. God will test your faith by allowing you to go through trials and tribulations because He knows that GREATER is on the inside of you and that He has already equipped you with everything you need to go through something.

Sometimes when you are going through hell and high water, and the fierce winds are seemingly blowing from every direction, causing stress, confusion and turmoil in your life, that is when you will hear that still small voice of the Lord speak to you and reveal to you, maybe even in a dream, "the blessing that is on the other side of that trial..." He will strengthen your faith by manifesting His promises in your life.

NIGHT VISIONS

A DIARY FOR YOUR DREAMS

~DREAMER'S DIARY~

_____

_____

_____

_____

_____

_____

_____

_____

_____

_____

_____

_____

_____

_____

_____

_____

~DREAMER'S DIARY~

_____

_____

_____

_____

_____

_____

_____

_____

_____

_____

_____

_____

_____

_____

_____

_____

~DREAMER'S DIARY~

_____

_____

_____

_____

_____

_____

_____

_____

_____

_____

_____

_____

_____

_____

_____

_____

_____

_____

~DREAMER'S DIARY~

_____

_____

_____

_____

_____

_____

_____

_____

_____

_____

_____

_____

_____

_____

_____

_____

~DREAMER'S DIARY~

_____

_____

_____

_____

_____

_____

_____

_____

_____

_____

_____

_____

_____

_____

_____

_____

~DREAMER'S DIARY~

_____

_____

_____

_____

_____

_____

_____

_____

_____

_____

_____

_____

_____

_____

_____

_____

_____

~DREAMER'S DIARY~

~DREAMER'S DIARY~

_____

_____

_____

_____

_____

_____

_____

_____

_____

_____

_____

_____

_____

_____

_____

_____

_____

_____

_____

NIGHT VISIONS

~DREAMER'S DIARY~

_____

_____

_____

_____

_____

_____

_____

_____

_____

_____

_____

_____

_____

_____

_____

_____

NIGHT VISIONS

~DREAMER'S DIARY~

_____

_____

_____

_____

_____

_____

_____

_____

_____

_____

_____

_____

_____

_____

_____

_____

_____

_____

~DREAMER'S DIARY~

NIGHT VISIONS

~DREAMER'S DIARY~

_____

_____

_____

_____

_____

_____

_____

_____

_____

_____

_____

_____

_____

_____

_____

_____

_____

~DREAMER'S DIARY~

_____

_____

_____

_____

_____

_____

_____

_____

_____

_____

_____

_____

_____

_____

_____

_____

_____

_____

~DREAMER'S DIARY~

_____

_____

_____

_____

_____

_____

_____

_____

_____

_____

_____

_____

_____

_____

_____

_____

~DREAMER'S DIARY~

_____

_____

_____

_____

_____

_____

_____

_____

_____

_____

_____

_____

_____

_____

_____

_____

_____

~DREAMER'S DIARY~

_____

_____

_____

_____

_____

_____

_____

_____

_____

_____

_____

_____

_____

_____

_____

_____

NIGHT VISIONS

~DREAMER'S DIARY~

_____

_____

_____

_____

_____

_____

_____

_____

_____

_____

_____

_____

_____

_____

_____

_____

~DREAMER'S DIARY~

_____

_____

_____

_____

_____

_____

_____

_____

_____

_____

_____

_____

_____

_____

_____

_____

_____

NIGHT VISIONS

~DREAMER'S DIARY~

_____

_____

_____

_____

_____

_____

_____

_____

_____

_____

_____

_____

_____

_____

_____

_____

ABOUT THE AUTHOR

Greta James was born and raised in Camden, Alabama. She now resides in Huntsville, Alabama. She is the proud mother of one daughter, Camille Miller. She enjoys spending family time with her daughter. She is a Christian woman who loves the Lord.

Greta is a graduate of Alabama A&M University. She holds a Bachelor's and Master's degree. She is an Educator who works in the Huntsville City

Schools. She is a first-time author who was inspired by God to write this book.

www.ingramcontent.com/pod-product-compliance
Lightning Source LLC
Chambersburg PA
CBHW051044030426
42339CB00006B/198